Blogging

Getting To $2,000 A Month In 90 Days

Isaac Kronenberg

owners themselves, not affiliated with this document.

Table of Contents

Introduction

I'm not here to make any outrageous claims that you can earn upwards of six figures straight off the bat with a blog, it takes some time to hit 6 figures, but instead I will lay out a strategy for you to get you from zero to making $2,000 a month blogging in 90   days.

Although you may be a bit skeptical, you're going to have to trust me that this works, because it most certainly does indeed work! As the strategies laid out in this book are not merely ones that have made me a successful blogger, but they're also the same strategies the top earning bloggers on the planet are using, and the reason that they use them is for the simple fact that these strategies work!

This book is, I would say, the most advanced blogging book on the market, that teaches nothing but the most up-to-date blogging monetization strategies to get you from zero to $2,000 a month in 90 days. This will be the best blogging book that you have ever read, with the one exception being my previous book. However, this is even better than my previous book if your goal is purely an ultra-fast way to get your blog paying you an income!

That said, you will be expected to put in 2 hours of work a day on things, so if you don't have at least 2 hours a day you can dedicate to your blog, then this book isn't for you!

This book is organized in progressive steps, where it is critical that you follow the steps in order, chapter by chapter, before moving on. The exception is Chapter 2 which is designed for beginners to get from nothing to being able to make blog posts on their own hosting platform, Therefore, if you feel you're not a beginner, then please feel free to skip chapter 2 and you'll be just fine.

I should note though, that if you already have a blog, then I would recommend making a new one for the purpose of this book, because what this book will be teaching you to build is not just any normal blog, but rather one of the most lucrative kinds of blogs that exist!

Though I should state that if you already have a large audience and can find a way to integrate the method in this book into your own blog (which should be possible for most blogs), then that might also work. However, if you find that this method just won't vibe with your current blog, then it may be high time for you to start a new kind of blog! I myself run many blogs, so it's definitely do-able.

I'm going to be honest with you and say that some people won't be able to get to $2,000 a month with the method described in this book, and those people are:
-People who deviate from this method and don't follow my instructions to the tee. You really do have to follow the method exactly as it is described and not deviate from it. I've run numerous experiments on it, had conversations with many a big money blogger about it, and I've personally split-tested every strategy in this book, and there's a reason why the method was designed as it has, because it's the most effective way to get a blog to the point of earning a profit out there. Therefore, please just show some trust in the method and execute on it without deviating. If you are able to stick to the method, you are sure to be   successful!
-People who dedicate 2 hours a day to their blog, but work at an extremely slow pace. If you work extremely slow, then it will take you a lot longer than 2 hours a day! This method is designed for those who are able to blog at a would-be normal pace and is not for the truly slow. That said, if you are truly slow at things or get things done in about half the time of what is considered normal, then you can still be successful, though it will just take you longer to get there than 90 days.

-People whose blog posts are so poorly written and illogical, that the writing could be described as garbage, atrocious, or at the same level of a 6 year old child. The fact of the matter is that blogging is writing, though you don't have to be an amazing writer to be successful at blogging. However, you do have to make sense and at least be able to write at a level of coherency where what you write makes sense and can be understood by most people.

I can hear some of you crying out in agony already: What is this load of horse-@#%^?! You said I'd make $2,000 a month, why did   you   lie   to   me?

I never lied to you, this method will definitely work, especially if you follow my instructions, work at a decent pace, and are able to write decent blog posts. Note that I'm not asking for excellence here, just a decent level of output will suffice. However, if your work is indeed excellent, then you should be able to by far exceed the $2,000 mark!

If you read my last book, you may find we're covering some of the same strategies throughout a lot of this book, for no other reason than the fact that they are the most effective strategies out there. However, I think you'll find that it's not all the same, as this book teaches you something very specific, which is how to get to $2,000 a month in a 90 day period which was never taught in my last book. Furthermore, we'll be building a very specific kind of blog in this book utilizing a proven method that I have never taught before. I'd also like to be clear on the fact that you needn't have read my last book to benefit from this one, though they do make very good companions.

Lastly, I should mention that as a special gift for purchasing this book, I'm throwing in a free WordPress plugin that will greatly help you with monetizing your blog. More information on that plugin can be found in Chapter 12 of this book. Note: If you bought my last book, it's the same plugin!

See you in the next chapter!

Chapter 0: Why You Won't Find These Strategies On The Net?

I'm a 40 year old former Fortune 50 corporate slave who decided to drop out if the rat race to blog full time. That said, years prior to quitting my job I put tons of hours into my blog and never made a dime.

It was only just prior to quitting my job that I figured out how to monetize things. And monetize I did, to the tune of replacing and exceeding my income.

I did it by studying the work of big money bloggers, talking to them about their monetization strategies, and compiling data on how they were able to monetize their blogs. Some of the ways in which they had their blogs monetized completely eluded me and it was only once I started pushing big money bloggers for answers to the puzzle that I had finally cracked the code, and then later fine-tuned and optimized it to work for me. I got my original blog and the many other blogs that I later started specifically with monetization in mind to make me a small fortune.

This book is the culmination of everything I have learned as it pertains to a specific set of strategies for getting a fully monetized profitable blog up and running fast! Everything in this book is based on the strategies that big money bloggers use, which simply work, and are the most effective strategies out there.

The strategies I teach are all proven, and everything has been tested numerous times by myself to ensure that this method could be implemented by anyone to create the most optimized, most monetized blog that is possible to create by a human being.

If there was a magic pill that could take you from nothing to earning a full-time income from a blog, then this book is the closest thing in existence to that magic pill.

You simply won't find this magic formula for monetizing in any kind of blogging tutorial on the Net, because anyone who knows this formula doesn't want to create competitors for themselves, and they're mostly too busy enjoying their wealth to even care about sharing how they got their blog to be so profitable.

So why did I decide to share this information and write this book you might be wondering? Why not just focus on my multiple blogs and relax on some island?

The simple answer is because I'm crazy! I enjoy dissecting how things are done and sharing it with people. I thought about just putting this whole method on one of my blogs, but a book seemed like a better delivery vehicle simply due to the sheer volume of information that would need to be relayed.

Sure, you might find some parts of my method in other blogging tutorials, but I have never seen the whole method published or written anywhere before, probably because no one has studied the big money bloggers as much as myself or endeavored to put all of their strategies for making the perfectly monetized blog in one book. However, if you analyze the big money bloggers or talk to them, you would find that most used either this exact method or some variant of it to get to where they are.

You should be thanking yourself for purchasing this book, because you just saved yourself the hassle of years of work and making tons of huge costly mistakes to be able to finally get your blog to the point where it's paying you an income!

It's all here, the fruits of my blood, sweat, and tears is now yours to reap and sow!

I proudly pass the torch to you, giving you the secret weapon you need to make a fortune in this blogging game. The exact book I wish I had when I was figuring everything out is now yours! And so you are a very lucky one indeed to possess this book!

Enjoy!

Chapter 1: Pick A Niche & Find Affiliate Programs For It

Since we're going to be focusing on a very specific kind of blog to bring you to $2,000 a month in 90 days, I'm going to give you some highly specialized blogging advice that is a bit different than the advice I normally give.

In case you didn't know, I normally just advise people to pick a niche that they are passionate about. However, with the kind of blog that we're going to be building, my advice is that you pick a niche that you are passionate about that also has a large amount of new products coming out regularly.

Examples of niches with lots of products coming out regularly include: digital cameras, notebook computers, golf clubs, video games for a particular platform, music composition software, etc.

Make sure you're passionate about the niche you choose though, as being passionate about your niche is a key component of this method. It's really hard to blog about anything you are not passionate about.

So if you're into vacuum cleaners, and quite passionate about them. Well, then I'd say you have a fabulous niche there!

Yes, in case you haven't figured it out by now, we're going to be starting a review blog, which means that we're going to be reviewing the products in the niche we choose. In fact, every blog post you write will be a product review, which is exactly why you'll need to choose a niche with lots of products coming out for it regularly.

Why are we going to be creating a review blog?

Well, it just so happens that review blogs are without a doubt the most lucrative kind of blog that a person can start. $2,000 a month is actually nothing for a well-built review blog. Therefore, if monetization is the game (and I'm assuming it is for you, since you did purchase this book with money all over the cover), then we want to start a review blog over any other kind of blog!

Now, before you start building anything, there is one more component, being that you want to start a review blog with products that have affiliate programs.

What's an affiliate program you say? Well, it's basically a program designed by a company that gives you a link or banner to a product's sales page, and if someone clicks on that link or banner and buys the product, you get paid a percentage of the sale. The mechanics of how it all works isn't important for the purpose of this book, but just know that there are affiliate programs out there for nearly every kind of product that you can imagine.

Amazon for example, has an affiliate program that covers nearly any product you can imagine. To check it out, search in Google for the keywords "Amazon Affiliates" and it should be the first link that pops up.

Though Amazon is just one example. You want to do a bit of research and find the affiliate program that pays the most, and by a company that focuses on products in your niche. Thus, you want to search Google for your product's name or some niche specific keywords followed by the words "affiliate program." If no affiliate programs can be found for the product or niche specific keywords you're searching for, and if not even Amazon carries your products, then it's time to find a different niche.

Note: The niche you choose doesn't have to have physical products, downloadable info products and downloadable software products are also fine, as long as your niche has plenty of them coming out regularly, and as long as affiliate programs for those niches exist.

I should also mention that one great place to turn for lots of niche specific affiliate programs are sites called affiliate networks. I've included a list of affiliate networks below (which is by no means a comprehensive list) that you can search for on Google, though you can also try searching for the keywords "affiliate networks" to find more.

JVzoo
Clickbank
CJ Affiliate by Conversant
Rakuten Marketing
Warrior PLus
Shareasale

There are tons more affiliate networks out there, so don't let my short list be the end-game. Whichever affiliate network you might choose to go with largely depends on your niche. I personally really like JVzoo and Clickbank for the stuff I'm into, but don't let my preferences limit you, as you want to do your own research to find one that fits best with whatever niche you've decided to go with.

If you've got a niche and you're passionate about it, and it has affiliate programs, then we're good! If not, then keep thinking about   it   until   you   have   one!

Do you have a good niche now? Well, great then!

Chapter 2: Domain Name, Hosting, and WordPress

As mentioned in the Introduction of this book, if you're no newbie to blogging, which means you have your own domain name, hosting, WordPress installed, and you can already write blog posts, then feel free to skip this chapter.

If you're still here, then I'm assuming that you are truly at the beginner level, so we're going to fix you by the time you've finished reading this chapter.

To start your blog you basically need 3 things, a domain name, hosting, and WordPress.

Since the market for hosting is always changing, it's hard to recommend you the best registrar or hosting provider (in regards to features, pricing, etc.), since what I recommend to you this week might not be the best deal next week. Therefore, I would like to direct you to a link where I'll be providing the most up to date information on what the best deal on the market is. Also, you'll find a link to a Wordpress tutorial there, which will have you up and running as quickly as possible, to the point where you'll be able to write blog posts. Just go to:

http://BloggerBlogger.com/Basics/

Note: To unlock this page you'll have to put in your email address which will add you to my list, though you can always unsubscribe. Although as part of my list you'll receive updates on the blogging industry, and info on new strategies and tools for making your blog more profitable, so it would probably be in your best interest to be on my list.

It may seem a little bit cold to just refer you to a website to learn to put up your blog and then wash my hands of you, but getting a domain name and hosting is something best done online, as is learning WordPress, thus it is in reality the quickest route to getting you up to speed! As most of what this book covers is getting your blog to a point where it is profitable and generating an income for you, which largely stems from a point after having achieved basic competency with WordPress. Everyone had to learn WordPress at some point to be able to write blog posts, and so you have to do that too. It's not hard though, you should have it down in less than a day, or if you're really quick in less than 15 minutes   is   entirely   possible.

I should also say that when choosing a domain name, pick anything that most closely represents the niche you chose and is memorable (meaning that if you told me the name over the phone,   I'd   be   able   to   remember   it).

Your domain name actually doesn't matter one smidge for ranking in search engines, so don't worry about that part of things   at   all.

Before moving on to the next chapter, you should have accomplished:

-Getting hosting and a domain name (possibly both from the same company).
-Installing Wordpress and figuring out how to write your first blog   post.

If you've done that, then congratulations! You're no longer a beginner, and thus we're ready to move on to the next chapter. See you there!

Chapter 3: Choosing Affiliate Programs

As mentioned in Chapter 1, you should have picked a niche with products that have an affiliate program.

What you want to do now is conduct further research in order to find the best affiliate programs that will pay you the highest percentage on the products that you will be reviewing. Make sure to read the terms of every affiliate program that you find, and make a list of affiliate programs and how much they each pay out.

Next, what you need to do is register for all relevant high paying affiliate programs. Registering for an affiliate program involves providing your contact information, mailing address, and most importantly your banking details so that you can be paid. While some companies have their own affiliate program on their website, affiliate networks are an entirely different beast with numerous affiliate programs all in one place.

The great thing about affiliate networks is that you only need to register once, which will then give you access to all of the affiliate programs that they manage, though you'll have to learn how to use their platform (all good affiliate networks will have tutorials and support for you on how to use their platform properly). And since money is on the line, you want to make sure you completely understand how to use their platform before you get ahead of yourself, so be sure to go through all of their tutorials and contact their support if you have any questions.

The main point here is that you're going to have to do a lot of research and you're going to want to compare percentages paid. This might mean that you'll have to find multiple affiliate programs, as well as find and join multiple affiliate networks to be able to do thorough research on the matter.

In the end you want to choose only the affiliate programs with the best looking terms that will pay you the highest percentage. Hence, be sure to make a list of what you find and compare.

While it's difficult to give advice on what percentage would be considered a good one, as a rule of thumb I generally don't deal with anything that pays less than 30% for digital products, and less than 5% for physical products, and while it's not a finite rule (as things largely depend on your niche and the price-point of the products in that niche), I highly recommend you keep it in mind.

One more thing you should know is that affiliate networks usually rank affiliate programs in their database by either something called a conversion rate (how well the sales page converts into sales) or something called EPC (earnings per click - which is almost the same thing as the conversion rate). Affiliate programs that rank high for either of these ranking systems are generally more likely to bring you sales. Also, you want to be aware of the refund rate, if an affiliate program has a 100% conversion rate, but has a 100% refund rate, then I wouldn't go with that. Logically, the ideal would be a 100% conversion rate and a 0% refund rate.

Aside from all of that, what should decide whether or not you you go with an affiliate program (whether you find it in an affiliate network or directly from the company that sells the product) should be how good you think the sales page is. If you find it so convincing that you yourself would buy the product, then you've got a winner! However, if the sales page looks like some horrid thing that would cause you to never in your right mind purchase the product, then you probably wouldn't want to touch it.

Cloak Your Links

One last point, unless it is specified by the affiliate program you choose that you shouldn't cloak your links (Amazon Affiliates is known for this), you want to cloak your affiliate links.

Cloaking your affiliate links means using a WordPress plugin like Pretty Link, you can find Pretty Link and many similar link cloaking plugins in the Plugins area of your WordPress dashboard. Once you're in the Plugins area, just click on "Add Plugin" there, and then search for the keywords "cloak links."

What cloaking a link means is changing the URL of the link from something that looks like a complex jumble of letters to something that looks like a link to a page on your blog. It just looks nicer (especially if you also put the affiliate link on your Youtube channel), though it doesn't really matter on your blog itself if you use words like "Click Here" instead of an actual link. However, the real reason to cloak your links is to organize them more than anything else, and if you ever wanted to post your links on some other website in the future, the cloaked link is generally easier and cleaner to work with than the raw link. An example of this would be if you needed to update where your link takes someone, you could just update the URL that your cloaked link goes to in one place, and all of your cloaked links wherever they may be would then take those who click on them to the new URL. This is especially awesome if an affiliate program or sales page of a product ever goes down or is updated to some other URL, because rather than having a bunch of broken links that you have to update everywhere, you can easily direct people to some other sales page that might interest them or to wherever the updated sales page is by simply updating your cloaked link one time in one place.

Anyway, for this method the only affiliate links we will put anywhere will be on our blog and on our Youtube channel, and so cloaking them is just for organizational purposes. After you post

90+ affiliate links or so, you'll start to realize why organizing them is so important.

If this all makes sense, then we're ready to move on. If not, then reread this chapter and try to internalize and apply everything stated here.

On to the next chapter!

Chapter 4: Writing Blog Posts

You want to write one blog post a day, and every blog post that you write should be a review of a different product in your niche.

In each blog post you should put your affiliate link 3 times throughout your post. Once at the top of the article (below your headline), once in the middle of the article (product name underlined with blue font once, so it looks like a link, and actually is a link), and once at the bottom of the article.

Your link at the top and bottom of the article should say something to the effect of: CLICK HERE TO CHECK OUT BLAH BLAH, where BLAH BLAH should be replaced with the name of the product. The bottom most link could also be a banner link, if the the affiliate program for the product offers a banner (many of them   do).

I should also say that you don't need to actually have tried the product to write a review about it. Some of you might be thinking that it might be a bit unethical to write a review about a product you've never tried, and it's true that it is definitely better to write a review about a product you have actually tried. However, a lot can be determined about a product based on the sales page of the product, and if it's lacking in some aspect that is apparent without purchasing the product or has some benefit over other similar products, you should mention this. Also, if you actually haven't tried the product, you should mention in your review that you haven't actually tried the product (this makes it ethical).

Believe it or not, the big money bloggers regularly write reviews on products that they've never even tried, and the vast majority of reviews that many of the big money bloggers write are actually about products that they have never actually tried and probably never will try (not because they can't afford them or get a free review copy, but mostly because they don't have time to try them all). As long as you mention you've never tried the product, but you understand the niche and do your proper research on the product (enough to understand the ins and outs), it's acceptable.

All of this said, you should definitely try emailing each company you plan to review a product on asking for a free sample of the product for the purpose of writing a review. They'll want to know your blog domain name, but if you're just starting your review blog you probably won't get it, but after 50 reviews or so (before the end of our 90 days), some companies should start giving you free review samples of their products (depending on your niche). The bigger your blog gets and the more reviews you write, the more companies will be willing to give you free samples of their products to review. Just make sure you actually email the company for each review you plan to write, as there is nothing that speaks authenticity more than being able to say that you've actually tried a product that you're reviewing.

Secret Advanced Strategy

A secret advanced strategy that you want to implement is to include a bonus if someone clicks on your affiliate link and buys your product.

The reason why you want to include a bonus is because after reading your review some people might not click on any of your affiliate links (terrible, I know), and might instead just open up a new tab and search for the product on Google and then buy it somewhere else.

Adding a bonus to your affiliate link can be tricky, but can be done through most affiliate networks. The process of adding a bonus to an affiliate link is different depending on the affiliate network. For an example of how to do this on JVzoo, just type the keywords "JVzoo add a bonus to your affiliate link" into Google and you'll be hit with a bunch of tutorials on how to do this.

If your affiliate network doesn't have anyway of adding a bonus to your affiliate link or if you're dealing with an affiliate program run by the company that makes the product, then there is another way to implement this strategy, which is to ask the buyer to email you their order number or even send you a screenshot of the order confirmation page and the email they used to purchase the product. You can then check with your affiliate program (usually somewhere after you login into your affiliate account) to then match the order number or email used to verify that the buyer did indeed purchase the product through your affiliate link, and then manually email them a link to your bonus.

The WordPress plugin that comes with this book is good for putting a time-limit on that bonus which you add, in essence creating a scarcity effect, which should help your conversion rate. See Chapter 12 for more information on this plugin.

Wait A Second Here, Where Do I Get a Bonus?

That's an excellent question, and my answer to you is that you make it. Your bonus should be something someone in your niche would find desirable. It could be as simple as a PDF report explaining some trick to using the product in question, or perhaps something clarifying some aspect of your niche that those in your niche would want to know, or it could even be a video how-to on something in your niche at some secret page on your blog that only those with the link can find. What's important here is that your bonus supplies value, and is something desirable. I find short guides work well as a bonus, but anything of value that you could create will do. For example, if my niche was blogging, a short guide revealing 10 ways to boost traffic to your blog might serve as a good bonus. I think you get the idea.

While the bonus isn't necessary, it will definitely get your conversion rate through your affiliate links up. Thus, you really need to create a bonus, and so it is a part of this method, since having a bonus could make the difference between making the sale and not making the sale, and you need to adopt every advantage you can get if you really want to win at this blogging game.

Thus, you want to put your thinking cap on, and come up with some kind of bonus you can offer, and create it!

One last point I should mention is that if your bonus is product specific, you won't be able to use it on the next review you write tomorrow, so it's actually better to have a bonus that's niche specific that you can reuse, and then every now and then create a product-specific bonus for the really exceptional products that you review.

On to the next chapter!

Chapter 5 - Why You Need Youtube

A blog that is truly optimized for SEO should be linked to a Youtube channel and vice versa.

What I suggest you do is that every time you write a review on your blog you link it to your Youtube review of the same product, which shows a hands-on demonstration of using the product, or at the very least a hands-on look at the product's sales page. Also, you want to put a link in your description below each Youtube video linking back to your review page on your blog and vice versa.

Thus, every time you write a blog post you need to make a corresponding Youtube video and have the two linked to each other.

You don't need to put your face on your Youtube videos, just point your camera at the product, or if the product you're reviewing happens to be software, then use a good screencasting software to record your computer screen while you use the software and talk about it. It's also completely fine to just use screencasting software to record you scrolling around the product's sales page while you talk about it.

Search in Google for the keywords "screencasting software" and you should be able to find one that will work for you. While you don't actually need it, screencasting software will make it a heck of alot easier to record reviews. It's entirely your call on this one.

One last thing, make sure each Youtube video you make is approximately 10 minutes long, as this is the sweet spot for ranking Youtube videos well. Don't worry if you make a bunch of

Youtube videos and have no subscribers at all, they will come eventually.

One last critical point, when you title your Youtube videos, put the name of the product followed by the word "Review" or you could also put the name of the product followed by the word "Review" and then the current year. So for example if I was reviewing Widget 55, then my Youtube video title would be either "Widget 55 Review" or "Widget 55 Review 2017."

As for your Youtube tags, just put keywords you think are relevant to your video, but don't worry about the tags too much, as they're not as important as the title or video length.

Lastly, if you've never heard of Youtube, just search on Google for the keywords "Youtube" and you'll find it.

I'm not going to teach you how to make a Youtube channel as Google (Google owns Youtube) has plenty of information on that for free online. Though you could type into Google "How do I make a Youtube Channel?" and you're sure to find a ton of tutorials on that.

In addition to a link in your description leading to your review on your blog, should you put your affiliate link for the product you review below your Youtube video? Yes, you should! And not only that, you should also mention the bonus (we talked about in the previous chapter) that they can receive if they buy through your affiliate link!

Furthermore, in addition to a link to your blog and your affiliate link in your description, you want a second affiliate link to the same product on your Youtube video, which stays in one of the corners of the video for the entire length of the video, because not everyone will scroll down to your description. Don't make it a huge box, just a little thing, so that it doesn't get in the way of your actual video. The link should say something to the effect of

"Click Here To Check Out Blah Blah" where Blah Blah is the name of the product.

To put a link on your Youtube video, you're going to have to learn how to use a feature of Youtube called "annotations." Again, Google has plenty of tutorials about it, but if in doubt, search in Google for the keywords "how do I put annotations in my Youtube videos?" and you'll find a bunch of tutorials that explain the process.

You might be thinking that blogging has nothing to do with Youtube, and that isn't making a Youtube channel in essence becoming a Youtuber? Well, your blog should be your focus, no need to take your Youtube channel too seriously (unless you really want to), what we're doing here is creating a secondary force of affiliate and subscriber traffic, as well as improving your SEO through interconnecting your blog with your Youtube channel, which will help your blog to shine!

Make the Youtube channel!

Chapter 6: SEO

To get your SEO straight, you want to register your domain name with Google Webmasters, and fill in as much information as possible   with   them.

Google Webmasters is a platform designed by Google, and its purpose is to make sure your blog is being properly indexed by Google's crawlers so that it can be properly found.

Just search Google for the keywords "Google Webmasters" and the first link that pops up should take you there.

One more thing that will give your SEO an edge is that you should also make a Google Plus account and link it to your blog and Youtube channel as well.

Just search Google for the keywords "Google Plus" and the first link that pops up should take you there.

Other than that, if you're posting one review a day (unique content written by yourself) as this method suggests, your SEO should be spot on!

Chapter 7: Choose Affiliate Banners

Even though you will make plenty of money off of the affiliate links in your reviews, you should put up some affiliate banners that show up regularly in your sidebar or footer, or both.

While these banners can be for anything you want, I recommend that they be for longstanding, high quality items in your niche that won't easily become outdated that you regard as being the best of the best.

You should be replacing these banners as they become outdated. Though the less you have to replace them the better, which is why affiliate banners for longstanding, high quality products work best.

Most affiliate programs should have affiliate banners for you, but if not, feel free to shoot them an email to ask for some!

However, it may be true that some affiliate products don't have affiliate banners of any kind, in which case just placing the link is fine, though there's nothing that attracts clicks more than banners, so aim for banners!

Chapter 8: List Building & Monetizing

If you've heard this all before, just feel free to skip this chapter, but if not, then listen up!

When I say list, I'm referring to an email list of your followers.

One of the most important steps in this process is a step called list building. While you can make a decent sum of money without even building a list. A list will take your blog a lot further, because it gives you another channel where you can hit all of your dedicated followers all in one place.

So how exactly does one build a list? Well, unfortunately it's not as simple as just putting a form on your blog asking for emails and saying "join my list!" Trust me, I've tried that strategy and most won't join if that's all you have going (maybe if you were famous it would work).

To get people to join your list, you have to offer up an ethical bribe in exchange for their email. What you give your follows should be something incredible that possesses a high degree of value to them.. In the old days way back when, I used to just give a PDF report containing highly valuable information, however these days I give WordPress plugins, because I believe they have a high degree of value.

However, a PDF containing a high degree of value works just fine, and a video containing a high degree of value also works. It really all depends on what your target audience wants and what you're able to give them. After all, it should be something valuable enough that they're going to be thinking that it's a no-brainer to give you their email for it. So you really have to put yourself in their shoes and decide if you would give your email for that, if not then you need something with a higher value.

If my niche was vacuum cleaners, I might put together a report showing a comparison of the top 5 vacuum cleaners which also reveals my top 10 vacuuming secrets.

Only you can decide what kind of ethical bribe you want to give (think of it as being a second bonus that you offer), but it's best to give something that over-delivers what your audience wants, as it's all in the name of giving our audience what they want, because without them you wouldn't really have much or a list now would you?

Anyway, in order to set up this feat you first of all need to think hard and put together something of value for your followers. Put your heart and soul into it!

Then the next step is to get yourself an autoresponder! There are hundreds of autoresponders out there and they each have their positives and negatives, and if you want to know what I recommend, just go to BloggerBlogger.com and check out my banners.

I recommend though that you once again search Google and type in the keywords "autoresponder" and see what's around. A good autoresponder should also be able to produce a form that you can put on your blog, either in your sidebar or as a pop-up.

I recommend putting this form in your sidebar at the top, so it can easily be seen, and since many have pop-up blockers these days a pop-up isn't really the best strategy anymore.

You want your form to clearly state what your offering. Or a more advanced technique would be to just put your own custom banner in your sidebar offering some free guide or report of great value, and when people click on the banner it takes them to a form, which is basically like a sales page, but with the main point being your form.

You want to set things up with your autoresponder so that when they input their email they are automatically sent an email with a welcome message welcoming them to your list (or it might sound nicer if you called it a newsletter), and a link to the download page of your free ultra-high value report. Or it could just be a link to directly download the report from a free cloud storage service such as Google Drive or Dropbox.

Yeah, it's not easy, but you only have to set this up once and never worry about it again while it does its thing on autopilot. Also, your autoresponder service's support should be able to help you with a great deal of your set-up on this.

The autoresponder is a necessity, because not only will it help you get your form up, but it will also help you message your list. As your list grows you'll need to be able to shoot one email and have it reach thousands of people, and a good autoresponder service makes that possible. And a really good one will allow you to send pretty newsletter-like looking emails.

Once you've got this going though, it's then time to start emailing your list, and I'd recommend emailing them 2 to 3 times a week, so you're not spamming them. Be warned, if you spam them they'll unsubscribe.

In your emails to them, tell them about some new product you reviewed and include a link to your blog post. That's pretty much all there is to it!

Yes, you're going to write one blog post a day and record one Youtube video a day, and email your list less than your posting, so only email your list on the better reviews that you do.

If you were able to set all that up, then we're golden, and you'll be seeing a cash flow coming in mighty soon!

On to the next chapter!

Chapter 9: Guest Posting

After you have written 50 blog posts (after 50 days), from the 51st blog post you want to start a new habit that you implement at the end of every blog post you write. And that habit should be sending one email to some blog in or related to your niche asking if you can write a guest post for them. Do this for the next 40 days, thus you'll be writing one email a day to other blogs for the next 40 days, assuming you can find 40 other blogs in your niche, but if not then choose blogs that are as close as possible to your niche.

Most of the answers you will receive to your request should be a "yes." Though you might get some rejections (which is good, because you don't want to be writing guest posts every day).

Writing a guest post on someone else's blog one day instead of writing a post on your blog will make a world of difference for your traffic and for your profits. The benefit of writing a guest post is that the post will still have your affiliate links (just write a normal review, similar to the last 50 you wrote), and it will give you exposure to a wider audience who are likely to discover your blog. Yes, you need to put a link to your blog in your guest post, usually at the end, and state that for more information of this kind they can click here to check out your blog. What this accomplishes is stealing some traffic from the blog you post on and sending those readers to your blog.

Why would a competitor approve you to write a guest post if it would steal their traffic? Well, because writing blog posts is hard, and every article posted on their blog would give their blog more overall traffic, so most in their right mind would welcome the opportunity.

However, some bigger blogs might want you to write your guest post and submit it to them, and then might reject your post after you've submitted it. Though this is not a waste, because if that happens, just post the article on your own blog as normal (and remove the link to your blog from the article).

One well placed guest post can send a stream of traffic to your blog that will explode your followers ten thousand fold, and by the end of 90 days you should have sent out 40 emails requesting guest posts which should result in about 10 or more guest posts for you.

Once again, we should only send one email a day, each to a different blog in a similar niche as your own asking for an opportunity to write a guest post, and this process should be done after the 50 day mark.

Yes, you're going to have to start finding other blogs in your niche and listing them out. One thing though, don't waste your time guest posting on blogs that seem smaller than your own. Ideally you want to write guest posts for blogs that are much larger than your own. The bigger the better!

One last benefit of guest posting is that it will work wonders for your SEO.

Chapter 10: Summing It All Up

If you implement all the strategies in this book, then after 90 days you should have: 90 blog posts with affiliate links, 90 Youtube videos with affiliate links and links to your corresponding blog pages, one or more bonuses for those who buy through your affiliate links, one really good ethical bribe to give to people who join your list, 40 sent emails requesting guest posts, have registered your blog with Google Webmasters and Google Plus, and have set up an automated list building system on your blog's main page.

If you did all of that, way to go, as you should already be earning commissions around or upwards of $2,000 a month.

That's most of the battle that most people can't figure out how to do.

All you need to do now is continue what you've started, keep posting, keep making Youtube videos, and quit your job.

Chapter 11: Your Business & The FTC

If you're not already aware of it, then please be aware that blogging is a business, which means your subject to registering a business, reporting your income to the IRS and all of that jazz.

You're technically not a business until you get your first commission and hear a ka-ching sound, but once that happens, you'd better make sure you get your business all legally registered which will be a different process depending on where you live. Also, be sure to report your taxes.

Lastly, you want to make sure you're in line with the FTC if you're in America or if not than your country's equivalent.

Note: The FTC requires you disclose affiliate links. Therefore, make sure you search Google for the keywords "FTC affiliate links disclosure" and read up on their guidelines if you're running your business out of the U.S. If you're located elsewhere then you might not have to worry about it, but again you want to check your local laws. Also, even if you're not in the U.S., if you're dealing with an affiliate program run by a U.S. based company, be sure to check their terms, as they may require you comply with the U.S. FTC and properly disclose your affiliate links.

While no one likes to hear this stuff, it has to be said.

On to the next chapter!

Chapter 12: Free Bonus

As a thank you for purchasing this book, I am giving you a free WordPress plugin, which can be found at:

BloggerBlogger.com/Bonus

Note: To unlock this page you'll have to put in your mail address which will add you to my list, though you can always unsubscribe. Although as part of my list you'll receive updates on the blogging industry, and info on new strategies and tools for making your blog more profitable, so it would probably be in your best interest to be on my list.

After you download and install the plugin, just click on the help section of the plugin and watch the video for instructions on how to use it.

This plugin works best when you are including a free bonus for an affiliate product that you have reviewed.

This creates a scarcity effect which prompts people to purchase the affiliate product quickly in order to be able to get the free bonus.

I've ran split tests on this plugin and the end results definitely show an increase in sales.

I've tried to find better plugins that do the same thing, but this is the most effective one that I've found, and so I really love it!

I hope you also recognize the value in this plugin and that it gives your review blog an edge over others.

If you join my list, then you are likely to see me use this very plugin to increase my conversions, so look for it when I use this strategy!

Chapter 13: Beyond This Book

MENTORSHIP PROGRAM

If you are interested in going beyond this book and taking things to the next level, or if you just want personalized advice, I do have a private mentorship program where I personally examine your blog and advise you on what you need to do to make it profitable.

Although this book is in actuality all you need, I do offer a mentorship program for those who want to ensure success.

My mentorship program however is limited to time-frames in which I am able to take on new students.

To learn more about my mentorship program, go to:

BloggerBlogger.com/Mentorship

Note: To unlock this page you'll have to put in your email address which will add you to my list, though you can always unsubscribe. Although as part of my list you'll receive updates on the blogging industry, and info on new strategies and tools for making your blog more profitable, so it would probably be in your best interest to be on my list.

Also, please note that my mentorship program is only for the most dedicated bloggers who want to take their blog to an extraordinary level of excellence, if you feel that this is you, then I am looking forward to mentoring you!

If you find I am not currently taking students, then you may email me directly and I'll be sure to get back to you with my availability.

Chapter 14: Support Request

If you felt that this book taught you something, and it helped you, then it would be greatly appreciated if you could leave an honest review.

Reviews help me to release more books, and thereby provide more updated information of this sort to you, also leaving a review is just plain good karma and contributes to the ecosystem, letting others know what you liked or disliked about a book, thus leading to the overall creation of better books.

I look forward to reading your review, and will take them as feedback in creating better books of this nature in the future.

Thank you for taking the time to consider this support request.

Chapter 15: Good Luck

We've come a long way in this book, and I have revealed to you everything I know in how to take your blog to being a profitable force to be reckoned with.

I really appreciate you taking the time to read this book and hope it serves you well.

Though the book is now officially over, this doesn't have to be a goodbye, because if you have joined my list through one of the links provided in this book you'll be getting updates from me on the blogging world, and on the latest techniques used by the big money bloggers which will give you the edge in your pursuit of growing a profitable blog.

I wish you the best of luck on your blog, and look forward to providing you with further quality content in my newsletter.

Until then, good luck!

Chapter Z: A Warning

Wait, wait, the book is not over! There is one last bit to tell!

Let me start off by saying if someone threw a warning at me like the one I'm about to throw at you, I would be thinking: "Why on Earth are you wasting my time with this hokey mumbo jumbo, of course I'm not going to do anything like that, of course I have positive goals for my blog other than simply monetizing it. The very fact that you're warning me about this is utterly ridiculous!" And if that's your mode of thinking, then feel free to skip this last chapter and get to working on your blog! However, if that's not your mode of thinking, then this warning is for you!

Many moons ago, one of my former students betrayed me and used the blogging knowledge that I bestowed upon him to create a new method for monetizing one's blog, a dark method.

This student of mine had no passion about anything, and blogged with hate about topics he was not passionate about, but even worse than that, he pretended to be passionate about them.

He twisted the proven method I taught with a different logic, an unclean logic culled from the shadows of an dark and disturbing alien dimension, and forged a dark path for blog monetization, a path that my he claims will lead one to a million dollar blog, but there's a small catch, which is the death of your soul!

I warn you now, if you learn of this method, do not go down that path! Just stick to the method in this book, which is proven, well-tested, and allows you to keep your soul.

I only warn you of this, because I've witnessed the damage that blogging with false passion can do to someone, as it has destroyed my former student, turned him into something else, something horrid. It's a fate I would not wish on my worst enemy.

Do not forget this warning! Do not go down the dark path of blogging embracing hate masked by false passion at the expense of your soul, even for a million dollars it's not worth it!

I only mention this, because this is not just about blogging, but it's about life. Think about your life story, who you are and where you came from. Whether your story up until now is a positive one or a negative one, you should consider how you want to be known going forward and what story you want to leave behind when things are all said and done.

Thus, you should definitely take the time to deeply contemplate just what you are trying to accomplish with your blog other than pure monetization. All the big money bloggers have a goal other than monetization, such as trying to help people solve a particular problem, and so it's good to consider a similar type goal that goes beyond simply monetization; this is the key you must wield in order to avoiding the dark path of blogging.

Basically though, in choosing to engage in the act of writing a blog and build up a following, you will be at some point be changing people's lives with every blog post that you write. Thus, people's lives are on the line, the future is on the line, and you're responsible for how it all goes!

This is no laughing matter, because every blog post that you write has great influence that extends far beyond the walls of your world! Yes, you are indeed responsible for the lives of your readers, and not only that, you are responsible for shaping the world! Thus, if your blog posts are drafted out of seeds of hate, then you might cause the world to plummet into a state of disaster; I'm talking wars, anarchy, and the transformation of the world as you knew it into an extremely deceitful and hateful place.

On the flip-side, if you blog with love and passion about what excites you, you contribute to the facilitation of good vibes throughout the globe, and are assisting other powers in the creation of a loving and magnificent world to be enjoyed and cherished by all!

What has all this got to do with monetization?
This has everything to do with monetization, because if you blog from the perspective of hate you are contributing to the creation of a hateful world, and it sure would be difficult to enjoy your money when everyone is trying to scam you, deceive you, and steal your wealth. Thus, it's much better to blog with a true passion for something and enjoy your wealth in a generous and bountiful world that loves you!

Heed my warning, and do not go down the dark path of blogging, because karma is an interesting creature indeed, and it's likely to come back around and bite you in the ass if you don't watch yourself!

With that said, go on your way now and implement the method you have learned in this book! The faster you get on it, the faster you'll reach the 90 day mark and start seeing an income, and a following! The blogosphere is waiting for you, it's yours for the taking, so take what is rightfully yours and grab your piece of the blogging pie!

May you be the one who's blog is the greatest of them all!

Made in the USA
Middletown, DE
18 June 2017